Catching Curveballs Again

Verse By Verse Empowerment

DR. MOJI

rback: 978-1-963539-14-1

cover: 978-1-963539-15-8

he United States of America

ng: May 2024.

DEDICATION

dedicated to all the college students that I have ever had. You have taught me a lot t
tion career as a professor. I have learned from you how to become more reflective than
our feedback as personal – about me. And to always remind myself and remember that
ters in the journeys we took together. My sincere gratitude goes to you all.

Adversity may cast shadows, dark as night,
But within each adult, a spark remains,
A power untamed, that forever sustains.

They learn to flourish, amidst life's strife,
To embrace their strengths, enhance their life,
From Seligman's wisdom, they're inspired,
To seek joy and gratitude, all they desire.

Within these verses, empowerment lies,
A roadmap to greatness, reaching the skies,
Young-at-heart of Jos, in your hearts it resounds,
The power of words, where hope abounds.

Catching Curveballs, a beacon of light,
Guiding your way, with all its might,
May each verse ignite your inner fire,
As you embrace life's challenges, higher and higher.

So, let the verses whisper to your soul,
In Jos, Nigeria, may dreams be whole,
Catching Curveballs, an empowering embrace,
For today's young-at-heart, a path to grace.

BLOOMING BEYOND: ABA'S RESILIENT RISE

In Aba, Nigeria, a plot untold,

Of growth through trauma, a journey bold,

Catching Curveballs, they rise above,

Nurturing strength, embracing self-love.

From the depths of pain, seeds are sown,

Rooted in inner strength, they've grown,

Youths of Aba, "Japan of Africa", with hearts so strong,

Transforming darkness into a triumphant song.

In the city's fabric, scars remain,

Yet hope persists, like an eternal flame,

Through shattered aspirations, they find their way,

Blossoming anew, with each passing day.

From broken fragments, they gather strength,

Embracing healing, going to any length,

Rebuilding spirits, piece by piece,

Finding solace in growth, finding inner peace.

Growth after trauma, a testament grand,

In Aba's youths, resilience shall stand,

Catching Curveballs, they overcome,

In their hearts, the power of the sun.

With every hurdle, they rise and soar,

Transforming pain into wisdom's lore,

Aba's spirit, a beacon of light,

Guiding others to shine, to take flight.

So let this book be their empowering guide,

To navigate trauma's stormy tide,

Blooming beyond, they'll find their way,

For in Aba youths, resilience holds sway.

RESILIENCE GROWTH: ENUGU'S TRIUMPH

In Enugu's embrace, a tale unfolds,

Of strength and courage, as it beholds,

Resilience growth, a journey untold,

Where wounds become wisdom, as hearts unroll.

Amidst the shadows that once consumed,

College students emerge, their spirits resumed,

From shattered ideals, they rise anew,

Transforming pain into a vibrant hue.

Enugu, the "Coal City", a city backbone strong,

Where healing triumphs over all that's wrong,

Within each heart, a seed is sown,

A Simurgh rises, once thought to be gone.

From depths of darkness, light breaks through,

As college students discover strengths they never knew,

They forge a path, resilient and bright,

Transcending trauma, reaching for height.

Resilience growth, a powerful force,

Guiding hearts on an uncharted course,

In Enugu's embrace, hope flourishes wide,

As wounds transform into lessons applied.

With newfound wisdom, they spread their wings,

Empowering others, the joy it brings,

Catching Curveballs, a testament true,

To Enugu's college students, their adaptability comes through.

So let this book be a guiding light,

Inspiring minds to conquer the fight,

Resilience grows in Enugu's core,

For today's college students, forevermore.

BEYOND THE MASKS: KADUNA'S PERSPECTIVE

In Kaduna, the "Crocodile City", tales unfold,

Of masks, we wear, stories untold,

Actor-Observer Bias, a lesson profound,

Unveiling truths where perception is found.

Beneath the surface, judgments reside,

As adolescents navigate the ebb and tide,

Through biases woven within their minds,

They seek the truth, where empathy finds.

Kaduna, Nigeria, a city of diverse embrace,

A tapestry is woven with every tribe,

Adolescents ponder the roles they play each day,

Seeking to understand, in their peculiar way.

They break free from the chains of assumption,

Unveiling truths with compassion's consumption,

From the observer's perch to the actor's stage,

They bridge the gap, dismantling the cage.

Beyond the masks, true connections ignite,

In Kaduna's spirit, empathy takes flight,

Catching Curveballs, they defy the norm,

Embracing others, with hearts that transform.

For in their hands, the power they hold,

To shatter biases, to be bold,

To see beyond the surface, with open eyes,

In Kaduna's adolescents, perspective lies.

So let this book be their guiding light,

To question assumptions, to fight,

Beyond the masks, a world they'll see,

Empowering others, setting hearts free.

BREAKING THE SILENCE: ADO-EKITI'S CALL

In Ado-Ekiti, the "Fountain of Knowledge", a fable unfolds,
Of the Bystander Effect, its grip take holds,
Catching Curveballs, they challenge the norm,
Empowering voices to rise and transform.

In moments of crisis, when silence prevails,
Teens of Ado-Ekiti, Nigeria, your courage unveils,
A call to action, to break the chain,
To shatter indifference, to ease others' pain.

Within each heart, empathy resides,
Yet the Bystander Effect seeks to hide,
But in Ado-Ekiti's spirit, a change is due,
To be an upstander, brave and true.

They step forward, lending a helping hand,
No longer bound by the bystander's stand,
United in compassion, they take their part,
Igniting a ripple of kindness from the heart.

Through awareness and empathy's embrace,
Ado-Ekiti's teens claim their space,
Catching Curveballs, they break the silence,
Unveiling the power of benevolence.

For in unity, they find strength and might,

To uplift others, to shine their light,

Ado-Ekiti's voice, loud and clear,

A beacon of hope, dispelling fear.

So let this book be their rallying cry,

To never stand idle as moments pass by,

Breaking the Silence, their purpose aligns,

For in Ado-Ekiti's teens, compassion shines.

UNVEILING BRILLIANCE: ONDO'S TRUE LIGHT

In Ondo, the "City of Palm Oil Production", a secret hides,

Imposter Syndrome, where brilliance subsides,

Catching Curveballs, they unlock the gate,

Empowering youngsters to embrace their fate.

Within their minds, self-doubt may arise,

A cloak of insecurity, veiling their skies,

But in Ondo, Nigeria, transformations unfold,

Unveiling true brilliance, as stories are told.

They journey within, to seek their worth,

Defying the doubts that plague the Earth,

In Ondo's heart, they find the key,

To unlock their potential, to set their souls free.

They shed the shackles of inadequacy's hold,

Embracing their talents, shining bold,

With each step they take, new confidence is gained,

As Imposter Syndrome's grip is restrained.

In Ondo's youngsters, authenticity thrives,

As they release the notion of living lies,

Catching Curveballs, they rise above,

Unveiling their brilliance, embracing self-love.

For they are unique, a shining light,

With gifts and talents, burning bright,

Ondo's true essence, they now embrace,

Radiating their brilliance, with elegance and grace.

So let this book be their guiding star,

To conquer self-doubt, from near or far,

Unveiling Brilliance, their journey so grand,

For in Ondo's youngsters, true greatness shall stand.

CONNECTED HEARTS: KANO'S DISTANCE DIVINE

In Kano, the "Center of Commerce" legends unfold,

Of social distancing, a challenge untold,

Catching Curveballs, they find a way,

To connect hearts, despite the distance's sway.

In times of separation, they learn to adapt,

Through virtual embraces, friendships unwrap,

Kano's forever young, resilient and strong,

Discovering unity, even when apart for long.

Though physical spaces may keep them apart,

Their spirits intertwine, forming a bond of heart,

Through technology's grace, they bridge the divide,

With messages of love, across screens worldwide.

They stand together, hand in virtual hand,

Supporting one another, across the land,

Kano's spirit shines, as connections grow,

In social distancing's embrace, their steeliness show.

Amidst the longing for hugs and shared spaces,

Kano's forever young, finds solace in virtual embraces,

Catching Curveballs, they empower the soul,

Finding strength in togetherness, as a whole.

For distance cannot dampen the human heart,

Nor dim the love that they impart,

Connected Hearts, their unity prevails,

As Kano's forever young, redefine distance trails.

So let this book be a testament true,

To the power of connection, no matter how few,

Connected Hearts: Kano's Distance Divine,

For in unity and love, in Kano, Nigeria, their spirits entwine.

SHAPING STARS: SOKOTO'S TRAIT MOSAIC

In Sokoto, the "Seat of the Caliphate", a mosaic takes form,

The Big Five traits, a compass to transform,

Catching Curveballs, they embrace each shade,

Empowering students to discover what's true.

Openness, the canvas of creative minds,

Imagination's playground, where brilliance finds,

Sokoto's students, with minds ever-expanding,

Exploring horizons, fantasies never disbanding.

Conscientiousness, the pillar of strength,

In Sokoto's students, it spans the length,

With diligence and discipline, they strive,

Unyielding in their pursuit, as fantasies come alive.

Extraversion, the flames that ignite,

In social bonds, their spirits take flight,

Sokoto's heart, vibrant and bold,

In connections they flourish, as stories patrolled.

Agreeableness, the foundation of care,

In Sokoto's embrace, empathy they share,

Compassionate souls, extending a hand,

Lifting others, across the land.

Neuroticism, the waves they ride,

In Sokoto, Nigeria, students' toughness is tied,

Weathering storms, they rise above,

Finding strength within, anchored by love.

So let this book be a starry guide,

To embrace the traits that reside inside,

Shaping Stars: Sokoto's Trait Mosaic,

For in their uniqueness, their brilliance shall speak.

RENEWAL'S GRACE: ZARIA'S COMPASSIONATE HEART

In Zaria, the "City of Knowledge", a weariness abounds,
Compassion Fatigue, its weight astounds,
Catching Curveballs, they face the toll,
Empowering young people to replenish their souls.

In a world of suffering, their hearts extend,
Yet amidst the empathy, a need to mend,
Zaria's young people, with a compassionate core,
Seek renewal's grace, to give even more.

For in the giving, there lies a strain,
Compassion's fire, flickering with pain,
But in Zaria's spirit, courage finds space,
To nurture their hearts, to restore their grace.

They learn self-care, to tend their flame,
To heal compassion's wounds, to reclaim,
To replenish their strength, through rest and reprieve,
So their compassion may continue to weave.

Zaria's young people, with wisdom they glean,
From the depths of compassion's serene,
They understand the importance, the need,
To tend to their hearts, their souls to feed.

With self-compassion as their guiding light,

They rise above fatigue, embracing the fight,

Renewal's Grace, they find the way,

To sustain their compassion, in Zaria, Nigeria, day by day.

So let this book be their tender guide,

To navigate compassion's ebb and tide,

Renewal's Grace: Zaria's Compassionate Heart,

For in their well-being, compassion shall chart.

ETERNAL SPARKS: PORT HARCOURT'S LOVE STORY

In Port Harcourt, the "Garden City", a love story begins,

Romantic flames ignite, as hearts undeniably spin,

Catching Curveballs, they chase the fire's gleam,

Empowering emerging adults to dream the love they deem.

Amidst the city's rhythm, love's melody resounds,

Two souls intertwining, in symphony profound,

Port Harcourt's emerging adults, with hearts open wide,

Embrace the magic of love's tender tide.

In stolen glances, in Port Harcourt, Nigeria, they find connection's thread,

Love's enchantment swirling, painting skies in red,

Port-Harcourt's spirit, a backdrop so grand,

As love's journey unfolds, hand in hand.

They traverse the landscapes, both familiar and new,

Exploring love's nuances, their hearts ever true,

With each beat, a promise, to nurture and protect,

Together they weather any storm they intersect.

Eternal sparks, they ignite and persist,

In Port-Harcourt's love story, they fiercely insist,

Catching Curveballs, empower the heart,

To chase love's desires, to choose their art.

For love knows no boundaries, no confined space,

Port Harcourt's emerging adults embrace its tender grace,

Eternal Sparks: a testament to Love's Might,

In their hearts, Port Harcourt's love shines bright.

So let this book be their guide and muse,

To navigate love's journey, to never lose,

Eternal Sparks: Port Harcourt's Love Story,

For in their love, emerging adults shall find glory.

THREADS UNRAVELED: ILORIN'S MEMORY MAZE

In Ilorin, the "City of Harmony", webs unfold,

False Memories, a tapestry of stories untold,

Catching Curveballs, they navigate the haze,

Empowering young individuals to unravel memory's maze.

Within the mind's corridors, illusions may reside,

Threads of recollection, where truth collides,

Ilorin's young individuals, with curiosity delve,

To distinguish the real from memories themselves.

False memories, like whispers in the wind,

They weave tales of moments that have been,

But in Ilorin's spirit, the power to discern,

To question the fabric, to seek what's stern.

With open minds, in Ilorin, Nigeria, they challenge the past,

Unraveling the threads, revealing what will last,

In pursuit of truth, their strength does rise,

Guided by wisdom, they see through the guise.

Ilorin's young individuals, brave and true,

They navigate the twists, the foggy view,

Catching Curveballs, they embrace the unknown,

Empowering themselves, their seeds of truth sown.

So let this book be their compass, their guide,

To trust their instincts, to let doubts subside,

Threads Unraveled: Ilorin's Memory Maze,

For in their quest for truth, their power shall blaze.

GLIMMERS OF GRACE: ABUJA'S GRATEFUL HEART

In Abuja, the "Capital City", a grateful heart finds a home,

Gratitude's symphony, where blessings freely roam,

Catching Curveballs, they count their blessings near,

Empowering youths to embrace gratitude's cheer.

Amidst the city's hustle, they pause and reflect,

On the gifts of life, on moments they collect,

Abuja's youths, with hearts wide open wide,

Embrace gratitude's essence, with joy as their guide.

In simple gestures, they find gratitude's glow,

In kindness received, in friendships that grow,

Abuja's spirit, a tapestry of grace,

As gratitude's light illuminates each space.

They savor the sunrise, the laughter's embrace,

The beauty of nature, each smile they trace,

With thankful hearts, they live each day anew,

In gratitude's embrace, in Abuja, Nigeria, life's colors come through.

Glimmers of grace, they scatter along the way,

In Abuja's youths, gratitude holds sway,

Catching Curveballs, they empower the soul,

To find gratitude's treasures, to make life whole.

So let this book be their reminder each day,

To find gratitude's blessings, come what may,

Glimmers of Grace: Abuja's Grateful Heart,

For in their gratitude, joy shall impart.

RHYTHM UNLEASHED: BAUCHI'S FLOWING SPIRIT

In Bauchi, the "Pearl of Tourism", a rhythm takes flight,

Flow's enchantment, igniting spirits so bright,

Catching Curveballs, they embrace the sway,

Empowering the young-at-heart to find their flow each day.

Amidst the city's pulse, they seek the zone,

Where time dissolves, and distractions are thrown,

Bauchi's young-at-heart, with passion deep within,

Discovering the magic of flow's vibrant spin.

In creative endeavors, they lose themselves whole,

As talents awaken, the barriers they unroll,

Bauchi's spirit, alive with rhythm's embrace,

In the zone they dance, with effortless grace.

With focused minds, they immerse in the task,

In the art of the moment, they fully unmask,

In flow's embrace, they find purpose so true,

Unlocking their potential, the skies they pursue.

Bauchi's young-at-heart, with rhythm as their guide,

They dive into the flow, where talents collide,

Catching Curveballs, empower the soul,

To find their unique rhythm, to reach their goal.

So let this book be their symphony's score,

To find their flow, in Bauchi, Nigeria, to soar and explore,

Rhythm Unleashed: Bauchi's Flowing Spirit,

For in their flow, the young-at-heart shall find limits unmet.

EMPOWERED VOICES: LAFIA'S ASSERTIVE STRENGTH

In Lafia, the "City of Solid Minerals", empowered voices rise,

Assertiveness unfolds, unveiling the wise,

Catching Curveballs, they embrace their might,

Empowering youths to stand up and ignite.

Amidst the city's rhythm, they find their voice,

With courage and conviction, they make their choice,

Lafia's youths, with strength deep within,

Discovering the power of assertiveness to win.

In respectful boundaries, they draw the line,

Expressing their needs, their truths intertwine,

Lafia's spirit, bold and unyielding,

In assertiveness's embrace, they find healing.

With clear communication, in Lafia, Nigeria, they navigate,

Through life's challenges, they emancipate,

In self-advocacy, their power does grow,

Empowered voices, seeds of change they sow.

Lafia's youths, with confidence they stand,

With assertiveness as their guiding hand,

Catching Curveballs, they empower the soul,

To assert their worth, to reach their goal.

So let this book be their guide to embracing,

The assertive spirit, with poise and grace,

Empowered Voices: Lafia's Assertive Strength,

For in their assertiveness, youths shall find their length.

THREADS OF CONNECTION: YOLA'S EMBRACE

In Yola, the "Land of Beauty", threads of connection weave,

Attachment's dance, where hearts do believe,

Catching Curveballs, they navigate the bond,

Empowering teens to cherish the connections they've found.

Amidst the city's embrace, they seek the ties,

In relationships nurtured, where love amplifies,

Yola's teens, with hearts open wide,

Embrace the power of attachment, side by side.

In family's embrace, a sanctuary they find,

A place of love and safety, forever intertwined,

Yola's spirit, in kinship's gentle hold,

They nurture attachment, as stories unfold.

With friends by their side, they laugh and explore,

Creating memories together, forevermore,

In bonds that strengthen, in Yola, Nigeria, in laughter and tears,

They find solace and support throughout the years.

Yola's teens, with compassion they share,

In attachment's embrace, they show they care,

Catching Curveballs, they empower the soul,

To cultivate connections, to make each heart whole.

So let this book be their reminder and companion,

To treasure attachment, to let love reside,

Threads of Connection: Yola's Embrace,

For in their attachment, teens shall find grace.

EMBRACING CONTENTMENT: MINNA'S INNER LIGHT

In Minna, the "City of Rocks", a shadow lurks unseen,

Envy's whispers echo, where hearts convene,

Catching Curveballs, they navigate the strife,

Empowering those youthful in spirit to embrace their life.

Amidst the city's sway, comparisons take flight,

Envy's grip tightens, dimming their light,

Minna's youthful in spirit, with wisdom they gain,

Learn to release envy, and break free from its chain.

In gratitude's embrace, they find their way,

Contentment's glow, where true happiness may lay,

Minna's spirit, resilient and strong,

They forge their path, where envy doesn't belong.

With self-acceptance, they celebrate their worth,

Embracing uniqueness, their gifts unearth,

In embracing contentment, in Minna, Nigeria, envy loses its hold,

Empowered by authenticity, their folktales unfold.

Minna's youthful in spirit, with self-love they'll grow,

Letting envy dissolve, their radiance show,

Catching Curveballs, they empower the soul,

To embrace their journey, to feel whole.

So let this book be their guide to empower,

To extinguish envy's flame, to let go and flower,

Embracing Contentment: Minna's Inner Light,

For in their contentment, those youthful in spirit shall shine bright.

UNRAVELING TRUTH: MAIDUGURI'S HONEST PATH

In Maiduguri, the "Land of Hospitality", the truth hides in the shade,

Lying's web weaves, where trust starts to fade,

Catching Curveballs, they seek honesty's embrace,

Empowering the zestful to tread on truth's righteous space.

Amidst the city's whispers, lies take their toll,

Duplicity's disguise takes their soul,

Maiduguri's zestful, with integrity they rise,

Choosing truth's path, where authenticity lies.

In transparent words, they find their strength,

Building bridges of trust, no need for pretense,

Maiduguri's spirit, resilient and clear,

They unravel deception, truth they hold dear.

With courage as their armor, they stand tall,

Defying the allure of falsehood's call,

In truth's embrace, in Maiduguri, Nigeria they find their might,

Empowered by honesty, their souls take flight.

Maiduguri's zestful, with integrity they'll thrive,

Guided by values, they keep truth alive,

Catching Curveballs, they empower the soul,

To walk the honest path, to remain whole.

So let this book be their beacon, their north star,

To choose truth's path, with hearts open wide,

Unraveling Truth: Maiduguri's Honest Path,

For in their honesty, the zestful shall find their worth.

BEYOND THE STORM: ILE-IFE'S SERENE MIND

In Ile-Ife, the "Cradle of Yoruba Civilization", worry's storm takes flight,

Anxiety's whispers, where shadows ignite,

Catching Curveballs, they seek tranquility's embrace,

Empowering the playful at heart to find calm in life's race.

Amidst the city's rush, worries may persist,

Clouding young minds, their wishes they resist,

Ile-Ife's playful at heart, with endurance and grace,

Discover the power to find a serene space.

In mindful breaths, they quiet the mind's tide,

Letting go of worries, finding peace inside,

Ile-Ife's spirit, resilient and strong,

They navigate the storm, where worries belong.

With self-compassion, they soothe their fears,

Nurturing their hearts, drying worry's tears,

In serenity's embrace, in Ile-Ife, Nigeria, they find their way,

Empowered by inner peace, worries shall sway.

Ile-Ife's playful at heart, with strength they'll rise,

Transcending worries, reaching for the skies,

Catching Curveballs, they empower the soul,

To conquer anxious thoughts, to take control.

So let this book be their guide on the hunt,

To find peace within, where worries can't infest,

Beyond the Storm: Ile-Ife's Serene Mind,

For in their tranquility, the playful at heart shall unwind.

REKINDLING THE FLAME: BIDA'S RESILIENT SPARK

In Bida, "Capital of the Bida Emirate", the flames flicker low,

Burnout's haze engulfs, where energies once flow,

Catching Curveballs, they seek renewal's embrace,

Empowering the joyful and carefree to reignite their inner grace.

Amidst Bida's demands, they strive and toil,

Drained by pressures, their spirits recoil,

Bida's joyful and carefree, with strength deep within,

Rekindle the flame, let resilience begin.

In self-care's sanctuary, they find their retreat,

Nurturing their souls, embracing rest's sweet beat,

Bida's spirit, resilient and true,

They reclaim their power, their goals anew.

With boundaries set, they reclaim their time,

Honoring their needs, replenishing their prime,

In self-compassion's embrace, in Bida, Nigeria, they rise,

Empowered by self-care, where burnout defies.

Bida's joyful and carefree, with indomitable will they'll rise,

Rekindling the flame, igniting their skies,

Catching Curveballs, they empower the soul,

To find balance within, to make themselves whole.

So let this book be their guide on the expedition,

To overcome burnout, to live fully blessed,

Rekindling the Flame: Bida's Resilient Spark,

For in their persistence, the joyful and carefree shall embark.

UNLEASHING POTENTIAL: CALABAR'S GROWTH WITHIN

In Calabar, the "Canaan City", the seed of potential lies,

A growth mindset sprouts, where imaginings start to rise,

Catching Curveballs, they seek a mindset's embrace,

Empowering university students to unlock their boundless space.

Amidst the city's rhythm, they nurture the seed,

Believing in their abilities, fulfilling their need,

Calabar's university students, with determination they'll thrive,

Embracing a growth mindset, where greatness arrives.

In challenges faced, they see opportunity's call,

Embracing failures as lessons, standing tall,

Calabar's spirit, resilient and strong,

They foster a mindset where possibilities belong.

With effort and perseverance, in Calabar, Nigeria, they unfold,

Unleashing their potential, shining bright and bold,

In the growth mindset's embrace, they let go of doubt,

Empowered by belief, they'll rise above and sprout.

Calabar's university students, with a thirst for knowledge they'll grow,

Embracing challenges, their skills they'll bestow,

Catching Curveballs, empower the soul,

To unlock their potential, to reach their ultimate goal.

So let this book be their guide on this mission,

To cultivate growth mindset, to be their very best,

Unleashing Potential: Calabar's Growth Within,

For in their mindset's growth, university students shall begin.

CHARTING INDIVIDUAL PATHS: WARRI'S INDEPENDENT BEAT

In Warri, the "Oil City", the bandwagon's allure,

A tempting dance where many hearts procure,

Catching Curveballs, they seek individuality's embrace,

Empowering youths to follow their own pace.

Amidst the city's sway, conformity may bind,

Losing their voice, their uniqueness confined,

Warri's youths, with courage they'll rise,

Embracing their path, where authenticity lies.

In self-discovery, they'll find their way,

Breaking free from the crowd's sway,

Warri's spirit, independent and bold,

They chart their course, their stories controlled.

With self-belief as their guide, they'll navigate,

Against the tide, their individuality won't abate,

In independence's embrace, in Warri. Nigeria, they'll stand tall,

Empowered by their choices, they won't stall.

Warri's youths, with conviction they'll explore,

Resisting the bandwagon's pull, forevermore,

Catching Curveballs, they empower the soul,

To follow their hearts, to reclaim control.

So let this book be their compass, their guide,

To break free from the crowd, to walk with pride,

Charting Individual Paths: Warri's Independent Beat,

For in their individuality, youths shall find their seat.

THE TAPESTRY OF SIBLINGS: IWO'S ORDERLY SYMPHONY

In Iwo, the "Home of Traditional Wrestlers", a tapestry of siblings weaves,

Birth order's melody, where each role achieves,

Catching Curveballs, they explore the family's embrace,

Empowering young ones to find their unique place.

Amidst the city's rhythm, sibling bonds prevail,

Birth order's story, where personalities set sail,

Iwo's young ones, with their birthright they'll define,

Embracing their position, where destinies align.

The firstborn, with leadership in their stride,

Shouldering responsibility, their presence amplified,

Iwo's spirit, nurturing and wise,

They forge the path, their siblings look to their skies.

The middle child, adaptable and kind,

Balancing the family dynamics, harmonies entwined,

In Iwo's embrace, they find their voice,

Supporting their siblings, in unity they rejoice.

The youngest, with a spark of spontaneity,

Infusing joy and laughter, their spirit free,

Catching Curveballs, they empower the soul,

To embrace their birth order, in Iwo, Nigeria, to play their role.

So let this book be their guide to understanding,

The beauty of birth order, like an orchestra's band,

The Tapestry of Siblings: Iwo's Orderly Symphony,

For in their birth order, young ones shall find harmony.

UNVEILING TRUTH: AKURE'S AUTHENTIC EMBRACE

In Akure, the "Sunshine City", authenticity thrives,

Unveiling truth where each soul arrives,

Catching Curveballs, they seek their voice,

Empowering young ones to make an authentic choice.

Amidst the city's rush, masks may appear,

Concealing true selves, hiding what's dear,

Akure's young ones, with courage they'll rise,

Embracing authenticity, where true power lies.

In self-discovery's journey, they'll find,

The essence within, their authentic kind,

Akure's spirit, genuine and bright,

They shine their light, banishing the night.

With vulnerability as their strength, they'll stand,

Embracing imperfections, reclaiming their brand,

In authenticity's embrace, they'll find their way,

Empowered by their truth, in Akure, Nigeria, they'll sway.

Akure's young ones, with authenticity they'll blossom,

Unveiling their colors, dispelling any gloom,

Catching Curveballs, they empower the soul,

To be true to themselves, to be whole.

So let this book be their guide to embracing,

The beauty of authenticity, their unique grace,

Unveiling Truth: Akure's Authentic Embrace,

For in their authenticity, young ones find their place.

METAMORPHOSIS: BENIN CITY'S EMPOWERED TRANSFORMATION

In Benin, the "Great Benin", a tale unfolds,

Self-reinvention's journey, where the eternally youthful beholds,

Catching Curveballs, they seek transformation's embrace,

Empowering themselves with newfound grace.

Amidst the city's hustle, they redefine,

Breaking free from old patterns that confine,

Benin City's eternally youthful, with strength deep within,

Embark on a journey where new chapters begin.

In self-discovery's realm, they'll explore,

Unveiling their passions, forevermore,

Benin City's spirit, resilient and bold,

They reinvent themselves, their stories untold.

With courage as their guide, they'll shed their old skin,

Embracing their potential, from within,

In self-reinvention's embrace, in Benin City, Nigeria, they'll rise,

Empowered by change, where their spirit flies.

Benin City's eternally youthful, with conviction they'll stride,

Transforming their lives, breaking barriers wide,

Catching Curveballs, they empower the soul,

To reinvent themselves, to reach their ultimate goal.

So let this book be their compass, their guide,

To embrace self-reinvention, to stand tall with pride,

Metamorphosis: Benin City's Empowered Transformation,

For in their self-reinvention, the eternally youthful find liberation.

UNBURDENED WINGS: ASABA'S RELEASE OF SELF-WORRY

In Asaba, the "City of Progress", self-worry takes flight,

A burdensome weight that dims the light,

Catching Curveballs, they seek liberation's embrace,

Empowering those with childlike wonder to free their anxious space.

Amidst the city's whispers, worries may grow,

Constricting young hearts, their spirits in tow,

Asaba's with childlike wonder, with strength they'll amass,

Releasing self-worry, like a bird from its grasp.

In self-compassion's haven, they'll find solace,

Untangling thoughts, finding peace in the silence,

Asaba's spirit, resilient and serene,

They'll break free from self-worry, a slate wiped clean.

With self-belief as their guide, they'll prevail,

Embracing the present, as worries they exhale,

In acceptance's embrace, in Asaba, Nigeria, they'll rediscover their might,

Empowered by letting go, taking flight.

Asaba's childlike wonder, with courage they'll soar,

Releasing self-worry, their spirits restore,

Catching Curveballs, they empower the soul,

To unburden their wings, to regain control.

So let this book be their refuge, their guide,

To shed self-worry, to let fears subside,

Unburdened Wings: Asaba's Release of Self-Worry,

For in their liberation, those with childlike wonder shall find their story.

26

THE INNER ORCHESTRA: OYO'S EMPOWERING SELF-TALK

In Oyo, the "Land of the Talking Drum", a symphony unfolds,

Self-talk's melody, where empowerment upholds,

Catching Curveballs, they embrace the inner voice,

Empowering young people to make a conscious choice.

Amidst the city's buzz, thoughts may sway,

Self-talk's power, guiding each step of the way,

Oyo's young people, with tenacity they'll align,

Harnessing self-talk, a harmony divine.

The conductor within, leading the way,

Nurturing thoughts, like a sunlit ray,

In Oyo's spirit, self-belief takes flight,

Transforming self-talk, a beacon of light.

With affirmations as their guide, they'll flourish,

Speaking words of courage, their souls will nourish,

In the orchestra of the mind, in Oyo, Nigeria, they'll compose,

Empowering self-talk, where confidence grows.

Oyo's young people, with intention they'll speak,

Harnessing self-talk, finding strength at its peak,

Catching Curveballs, they empower the soul,

To sculpt empowering thoughts, to take control.

So let this book be their anthem, their guide,

To embrace empowering self-talk, to abide,

The Inner Orchestra: Oyo's Empowering Self-Talk,

For in their self-talk, young people find their inner rock.

27

AWAKENING STILLNESS: IBADAN'S MINDFUL SOUL

In Ibadan, the "City of Brown Roofs", a mindful breeze whispers,

Awakening stillness, where presence glistens,

Catching Curveballs, they seek mindfulness's embrace,

Empowering young adults to find peace in life's chase.

Amidst the city's hustle, they find the space,

To breathe in the moment, to slow life's pace,

Ibadan's young adults, with awareness they'll thrive,

Embracing mindfulness, where inner peace arrives.

In quiet reflection, they discover the power,

To anchor their minds in the present hour,

Ibadan's young adults, serene and sublime,

They cultivate mindfulness, transcending time.

With open hearts, they embrace each sensation,

Tuning in to the beauty of their creation,

In mindfulness's embrace, in Ibadan, Nigeria, they find clarity,

Empowered by awareness, they unlock their ability.

Ibadan's young adults, with presence they'll flow,

Letting go of worries, letting their inner light glow,

Catching Curveballs, they empower the soul,

To live in the now, to be fully whole.

So let this book be their guide to exploring,

The depths of mindfulness, to cherish and adore,

Awakening Stillness: Ibadan's Mindful Soul,

For in their presence, young adults shall find their role.

28

DANCING WITH THE WIND: THRILL-SEEKING IN IDANRE

In Idanre, the "Home of Peace", where hopes collide,

A tapestry of souls, adventure's pride,

The young and young-at-heart, their spirits soar,

Catching curveballs, seeking something more.

Bold spirits rise with the morning sun,

As laughter dances, wild and fun,

In the city's bustling, vibrant throng,

They chase the thrill, where they belong.

Their hearts, like kites, against the breeze,

Embrace the challenge, their fears appease,

On dusty streets, they find their call,

Embodying courage, breaking free from the thrall.

Amidst the arid lands, they take flight,

Embracing life's adventures with all their might,

In the face of fear, they stand tall,

Writing tales of wonder on destiny's wall.

From dunes of doubt to mountains high,

They test their wings, they touch the sky,

United in spirit, in Idanre, Nigeria, they conquer and seek,

In the playground of life, they're daring and unique.

Through trials and triumphs, they endure,

Their joy infectious, their hearts secure,

Idanre's heartbeat echoes their desire,

To spark the embers and ignite the fire.

In Idanre's streets, aims unite,

Their verses empowering, their spirits alight,

Young and young-at-heart, their journey starts,

Dancing with the wind, as thrill-seekers' hearts.

So let this book be their guide to find,

Inspiration and courage, intertwined,

In Catching Curveballs, may they explore,

The boundless thrills that life has in store.

29

HARMONY'S EMBRACE: EMOTIONAL INTELLIGENCE IN ABEOKUTA

In Abeokuta, the "City Under the Rock", where pursuits take flight,

Emotions bloom in wisdom's light,

For the young and young-at-heart, a gift untold,

Catching curveballs, emotions controlled.

With hearts attuned, they seek to see,

Beyond the veil of what might be,

Empathy's touch, a gentle art,

In understanding, they find their part.

In joy and sorrow, they connect,

Embracing feelings, no aspect unchecked,

Through highs and lows, they navigate,

Emotional intelligence, their steady trait.

In Abeokuta's grace, they learn to share,

Their feelings woven, a tapestry rare,

With courage to express, they find release,

And forge connections, a lasting peace.

Amidst life's trials, they stand their ground,

With self-awareness, strength is found,

In conflict's dance, in Abeokuta, Nigeria, they seek a way,

To find solutions, and still, hearts sway.

In Abeokuta's realm, emotions take flight,

In harmony's embrace, their spirits ignite,

Young and young-at-heart, their journey unfolds,

With emotional intelligence, they'll catch all life holds.

So let this book be their clarion call and guide,

The essence of hearts, compassionate and kind,

In Catching Curveballs, may they explore,

The depths of emotions, to cherish and adore.

30

THE PHOENIX WITHIN: EMBRACING FAILURE IN ONITSHA

In Onitsha, "The Gateway to Eastern Nigeria", where ambitions reside,

Through twists and turns, life's turbulent ride,

For the young and young-at-heart, a truth untold,

Catching curveballs, failure's tales behold.

In the shadow of defeat's darkened veil,

Lies an opportunity, a hidden trail,

To rise again from ashes charred,

Failure's lesson, their hearts regard.

In setbacks faced and longings deferred,

Perseverance blooms, their spirits stirred,

For in each fall, they find the strength,

To rebuild longings of boundless length.

Through doubt and fear, they dare to leap,

In the face of failure, in Onitsha, Nigeria, they rise and reap,

The wisdom born from every fall,

A chance to rise, to give their all.

In Onitsha's streets, they stand tall,

Accepting failure as part of life's call,

With courage and grace, they strive to be,

The phoenix within, soaring free.

In Onitsha's embrace, their spirits ignite,

In the dance with failure, they'll find their light,

Young and young-at-heart, they'll bravely enthrall,

Embracing failure, to conquer life's thrall.

So let this book be their guide to success,

The beauty in failure, to realign,

In Catching Curveballs, may they explore,

The power within, to rise and soar.

31

UNRAVELING TRUTH: OVERCOMING GASLIGHTING IN OKENE

In Okene," The Home of Harmony", where hearts reside,

A darkness creeps in, where truth is denied,

For the young and young-at-heart, a caution foretold,

Catching curveballs, gaslighting's grips unfold.

In subtle whispers, doubts take flight,

A web of lies, woven tight,

But in their souls, a strength prevails,

To break free from deceptive tales.

Gaslight's flame may flicker strong,

Yet they'll question, where they belong,

With clarity, they'll find their ground,

And heal the wounds, deceit had found.

In Okene's embrace, they'll rise above,

The manipulation, the push and shove,

With confidence, they'll trust their voice,

Reclaiming truth, their hearts rejoice.

From shadows cast, they'll step into the light,

No longer blinded, their spirit's flight,

The power within, in Okene, Nigeria, they will reclaim,

To overcome, rise above the game.

In Okene's haven, they'll break the mold,

Their spirits strong, their hearts consoled,

Young and young-at-heart, they'll stand tall,

Unraveling gaslighting's thrall.

So let this book be their guide to find,

The strength to face the twisted mind,

In Catching Curveballs, may they explore,

The path to truth, forevermore.

32

EMPATHY'S SYMPHONY: HARMONIZING HEARTS IN LAGOS

In Lagos, "The Center of Excellence", where fancies entwine,

Empathy's essence, a gift divine,

For the young and young-at-heart, a tale to impart,

Catching curveballs, compassion's art.

In crowded streets, where lives collide,

They'll learn to walk, not just beside,

But in the shoes of those they meet,

To understand, to share, to greet.

With open hearts, they'll lend an ear,

To whispered joys and cries of fear,

In empathy's embrace, they'll find,

A bond that gently heals the mind.

In Lagos' heart, they'll see the pain,

The struggles, tears, and fancies that wane,

With kindness, they'll extend a hand,

To lift each other's spirits grand.

From every culture, every face,

They'll learn the power of love's embrace,

In unity, they'll bridge divides,

Where empathy is, grace abides.

In Lagos' rhythm, their spirits unite,

With empathy's power, their souls alight,

Young and young-at-heart, they'll truly see,

A world transformed, where love runs free.

So let this book be the key to guiding and igniting,

A symphony of souls, in Lagos, Nigeria, shining bright,

In Catching Curveballs, may they impart,

Empathy dances in every heart.

33

FINDING CALM AMIDST THE STORM: CONQUERING STRESS IN UYO

In Uyo, "The Land of Promise", where imaginations are bright,

A battle brews, within the night,

For the young and young-at-heart, quests unfold,

Catching curveballs, stress's grip they'll hold.

In whirlwinds of worry, they'll find their way,

Through stress and strain, come what may,

With strength in their hearts, they'll brave the tide,

And learn to breathe, to let stress subside.

In Uyo's tranquil spaces, they'll seek reprieve,

To ease the mind, to truly believe,

That amidst the chaos, they'll find a light,

A sense of peace, in the darkest night.

With mettle, in Uyo, Nigeria, they'll face each storm,

Learning to transform, to truly transform,

Stress into power, to push ahead,

In their hearts, courage will be bred.

In moments of doubt, they'll find their grace,

Embracing challenges they'll bravely face,

For stress may knock, but they will stand,

Uyo's strength guides their hand.

In Uyo's embrace, they'll conquer the quest,

To find serenity, to live their best,

Young and young-at-heart, their spirits will soar,

Catching curveballs, stress they'll ignore.

So let this book be a sanctuary of peace,

A guiding star that'll never cease,

In Catching Curveballs, may they find,

The calm within, the strength to bind.

34

WHISPERS OF THE HEART: EMBRACING INTUITION IN IKORODU

In Ikorodu, "The I-Town", where reveries ignite,

A voice within, shining bright,

For the young and young-at-heart, a power untold,

Catching curveballs, intuition's stronghold.

In quiet moments, a gentle call,

A whisper, a nudge, within the soul,

Their intuition, a guiding light,

A compass true, in the darkest night.

Through uncertainty's haze, they'll find their way,

In Ikorodu's grace, they'll seize the day,

With courage to follow what their hearts say,

They'll navigate life's mysterious array.

In trusting themselves, in Ikorodu, Nigeria, they'll forge a path,

Defying norms, escaping life's wrath,

Their intuition, a friend so dear,

Leading the way when choices are unclear.

In the bustling streets of Ikorodu's embrace,

They'll listen closely, embrace its grace,

For intuition's gift, a treasure to keep,

Through every challenge, their souls will leap.

In Ikorodu's realm, their spirits will soar,

Intuition's wisdom, they'll explore,

Young and young-at-heart, they'll find their way,

Catching curveballs, come what may.

So let this book be the lantern they'll wield,

To guide and illuminate their intuition's yield,

In Catching Curveballs, may they find,

Their inner compass, ever kind.

35

CHASING RAINBOWS: EMBRACING HAPPINESS IN BAMA

In Bama, "The 14-Ward Local Government Area", where thoughts unite,

A symphony of joy, a pure delight,

For the young and young-at-heart, a truth foretold,

Catching curveballs, happiness does unfold.

In laughter's echoes, they'll find their way,

Bathing in the sunshine, each passing day,

Amidst life's trials, they'll seek the light,

Embracing happiness, shining so bright.

Through fields of hope and skies so blue,

In Bama's heart, their objectives pursue,

With grateful hearts, they'll count their bliss,

Each moment treasured, a sweet caress.

In kindness sown, they'll reap the joy,

Spreading love,pn Bama, Nigeria, a radiant ploy,

For happiness thrives in selfless grace,

A gift to cherish, in life's embrace.

In friendships forged, they'll share the lee,

In unity, they'll dance with glee,

Their hearts aglow, like stars that gleam,

In Bama's realm, a happiness dream.

In Bama's haven, happiness will soar,

With open arms, they'll cherish more,

Young and young-at-heart, their spirits high,

Catching curveballs, reaching for the sky.

So let this book be their guide to ignite,

A tapestry of happiness, woven bright,

In Catching Curveballs, may they find,

The secret to joy, their hearts aligned.

36

RISING STRONG: EMBRACING REJECTION IN NSUKKA

In Nsukka, the "University Town", where projects may stall,

Rejection's shadow, a daunting thrall,

For the young and young-at-heart, a lesson foretold,

Catching curveballs, unyielding spirit they'll uphold.

In moments of doubt, they'll face the fall,

But through the pain, they'll stand up tall,

For in rejection's sting, they'll find their might,

To rise again, to shine so bright.

Amidst the whispers of uncertainty's call,

They'll seek their worth, not take the fall,

With hearts held high, in Nsukka, Nigeria, they'll dare to dream,

Knowing rejection's not the final theme.

In Nsukka's streets, they'll learn to grow,

To let rejection's winds, a new direction show,

For in each "no," they'll find a door,

To opportunities, they'll explore.

Through setbacks faced and projects deferred,

They'll persevere, undeterred,

Rejection's sting, they'll bravely embrace,

And find the strength to run the race.

In Nsukka's embrace, they'll rise and stand,

With courage strong, they'll grasp each hand,

Young and young-at-heart, their spirits soar,

Catching curveballs, they'll strive for more.

So let this book be their guiding light,

In every rejection, to see the flight,

In Catching Curveballs, may they find,

Unyielding spirit's grace, forever intertwined.

37

UNYIELDING RADIANCE: EMBRACING SELF-WORTH IN SULEJA

In Suleja, "The City of Rocks", where ideas invite,

A tale of worth, a shimmering light,

For the young and young-at-heart, a truth to hold,

Catching curveballs, self-worths unfold.

In the mirror's gaze, they'll find their grace,

A soul adorned with love's embrace,

No matter the doubts that may persist,

In Suleja's heart, they'll persist.

Through storms that rage and winds that howl,

They'll stand tall, their spirits avow,

In self-compassion, they'll heal and grow,

And see their worth, like sunsets glow.

In Suleja's streets, they'll claim their space,

Embracing every flaw, with an open embrace,

For in self-acceptance, they'll find the key,

To unlock the doors, to set their spirits free.

No judgment's weight will hold them down,

In their hearts, a resilient crown,

They'll rise above, in Suleja, Nigeria, like the morning sun,

In self-worth's glow, their battles won.

In Suleja's haven, their spirits soar,

Self-worth's essence, they'll adore,

Young and young-at-heart, they'll find their way,

Catching curveballs, where love will stay.

So let this book be a guiding ray,

An empowering gift, come what may,

In Catching Curveballs, may they see,

Their worth's brilliance, forever decree.

38

MIRROR OF GRACE: EMBRACING BODY IMAGE IN OGBOMOSHO

Ogbomosho, the city of unique "*Koso* Drums", where histories mold,

A journey of acceptance, a story untold,

For the young and young-at-heart, a truth to confide,

Catching curveballs, body image unified.

In reflections gazed upon with care,

They'll find beauty's essence, everywhere,

No matter the shape or size they see,

In Ogbomosho's heart, they'll believe they're free.

Through media's gaze and societal norms,

They'll challenge ideals, create their forms,

For in self-love's embrace, they'll find their might,

A radiant glow, in Ogbomosho, Nigeria, like stars in the night.

In Ogbomosho's streets, they'll stand tall,

Embracing their bodies, flaws and all,

With compassion's touch, they'll heal the pain,

And dance with joy in the summer rain.

No longer confined by beauty's chains,

They'll break free, releasing their pains,

In unity, they'll rise and shine,

Embracing bodies, divine and fine.

In Ogbomosho's realm, their spirits soar,

Body image embraced, they'll adore,

Young and young-at-heart, they'll find their way,

Catching curveballs, where self-love will stay.

So let this book be a guide and mirror of grace,

A sanctuary where love finds its place,

In Catching Curveballs, may they see,

Their body's beauty, unconditionally.

39

HEALING WINGS: EMBRACING FORGIVENESS IN POTISKUM

In Potiskum, the city of "Pots", where visions delight,

A path of healing, a beacon of light,

For the young and young-at-heart, a choice to behold,

Catching curveballs, forgiveness untold.

In the depths of hurt, they'll seek release,

A balm of forgiveness, a gift of peace,

In letting go, they'll find the strength,

To mend the wounds, to go the length.

Through battles fought and scars that remain,

They'll rise above the weight of pain,

With hearts unburdened, they'll leap,

Toward forgiveness' embrace, forever to keep.

In Potiskum's streets, they'll bridge the divide,

Setting aside grudges, letting go of pride,

For in forgiveness' dance, they'll find,

A chance to heal, a chance to bind.

No longer prisoners of anger's might,

They'll free their souls, like birds in flight,

In unity, in Potiskum, Nigeria, they'll find their place,

Hearts intertwined, in love's embrace.

In Potiskum's embrace, their spirits soar,

With hearts unshackled, they'll love once more,

Young and young-at-heart, they'll find their way,

Catching curveballs, forgiveness will stay.

So let this book be a guiding light,

A map of forgiveness, burning bright,

In Catching Curveballs, may they see,

The power to heal, to truly be free.

40

WINGS OF LAUGHTER: EMBRACING HUMOR IN JALINGO

In Jalingo, the "Sunshine City", where yearnings abide,

A tapestry of laughter, a joyous ride,

For the young and young-at-heart, a treasure to hold,

Catching curveballs, humor's sagas unfold.

In every giggle, they'll find their grace,

A remedy for life's chaotic chase,

With humor's touch, they'll conquer fears,

And dry the trails of sorrow's tears.

Through wit and banter, they'll connect,

In Jalingo's heart, laughter's effect,

For in every joke, a bridge they'll build,

A union of souls, forever fulfilled.

In the face of trials, they'll find relief,

A respite from pain, a joyous belief,

With laughter's echo, they'll rise above,

A symbol of strength, in Jalingo, Nigeria, a testament of love.

No matter how tough life may seem,

They'll find the light, like a radiant beam,

In humor's realm, they'll take their flight,

Their spirits lifted, shining so bright.

In Jalingo's realm, they'll dance with glee,

With humor's wings, forever free,

Young and young-at-heart, they'll find their way,

Catching curveballs, where laughter will sway.

So let this book be their guide to explore,

A world of laughter, an endless encore,

In Catching Curveballs, may they see,

The magic of humor, forever carefree.

EPILOGUE

rts, Empowering Souls

the final pages of "Catching Curveballs Again: Verse By Verse Empowerment,"
grateful for this poetic journey we've shared. Through the prism of Nigerian cities, v
motions, challenges, and triumphs, each collage of verses a glimmering thread w
shared human experience.

vere crafted to reach not only the young, who may be navigating the often turbulent w
also those young at heart, seeking solace, guidance, and inspiration regardless of ag

mbrace the topics that often linger in the shadows, waiting for the light of understa
our willingness to embark on this journey with me warms my heart.

flowed onto these pages, it became clear that the power of poetic expression exten
as. It offers a haven for reflection, a sanctuary for self-discovery, and a springboard
ve explored growth after trauma, the courage to break the silence, the triumph of e
f-worth, and the transformative power of forgiveness, among many other themes.

of verses has been a brushstroke on the canvas of empowerment. Together, they
ortitude, a chorus of assertiveness, and a gallery of compassionate hearts. I hope tha
found echoes of your own experiences, your aspirations, and your strength.

is book, I encourage you to carry these verses of empowerment with you. Let them
rough life's curveballs, a lighthouse in moments of darkness, and a reminder that
ourney. Embrace the bounce-back ability, the wisdom, and the beauty within you, fo
t we uncover our true strength.

ses continue to inspire, empower, and uplift you. May they remind you that you a
y storm, of finding light amidst shadows, and of embracing the extraordinary within

allowing these verses to touch your heart. Keep them as a treasure, a testament to
d remember that the power to shape your story resides within you. As you venture f
rveballs again and again with grace, vigor, and the unwavering knowledge that yc
uable – it shall be so.

and hope,